The Aquinas Lecture, 1965

THE UNIVERSITY IN PROCESS

Under the Auspices of Wisconsin-Alpha
Chapter of Phi Sigma Tau

by

JOHN O. RIEDL, PH.D.

MARQUETTE UNIVERSITY PRESS
MILWAUKEE
1965

Library of Congress Catalog Card Number 65-19126

© Copyright 1965
By the Wisconsin-Alpha Chapter
of the Phi Sigma Tau
Marquette University

To

Clare

Prefatory

The Wisconsin-Alpha Chapter of Phi Sigma Tau, the National Honor Society for Philosophy at Marquette University, each year invites a scholar to deliver a lecture in honor of St. Thomas Aquinas whose feast day is March 7. These lectures are customarily given on the first or second Sunday of March.

The 1965 Aquinas Lecture "The University in Process" was delivered on March 7 in the Peter A. Brooks Memorial Union of Marquette University by Dr. John O. Riedl, Professor of Philosophy, Marquette University.

Professor Riedl was born in Milwaukee on June 10, 1905. He earned the A.B. at Marquette University in 1927 and the M.A. the following year. In 1930 he received the Ph.D. Post-doctoral studies were made at the University of Toronto, Columbia University, and the University of Breslau, Germany.

Professor Riedl began his teaching career at Marquette University and was

Associate Professor of Philosophy in 1942, when he was on leave of absence for service in the United States Navy. In 1946 he became Chief of Catholic Affairs, Office of Military Government for Germany; then in 1949 Chief of Education Branch in the Office of U.S. High Commissioner for Germany. Dr. Riedl returned in 1954 to Marquette University as Professor of Philosophy and Dean of the Graduate School. Since 1960 he has given his full time to teaching Philosophy.

Beginning in 1935, when he was elected president of the American Catholic Philosophical Association, Professor Riedl has been active in higher education as member of the Catholic Commission on Intellectual and Cultural Affairs (since 1947), as member of Committee on Citizen Consultations, U.S. National Commission for UNESCO (1957-1961), as member of Commission on Educational Organizations, National Conference of Christians and Jews (1957-1961), as member of Board of Foreign Scholarships, Department of State (1958-1963).

His publications include: A *Catalogue of Renaissance Philosophers* (Milwaukee: Marquette University Press, 1940); translation of Josef Koch's *Giles of Rome: Errores Philosophorum* (Milwaukee: Marquette University Press, 1944); chapters in four books; articles in *The New Scholasticism* and *Proceedings, American Catholic Philosophical Association.*

To this list Phi Sigma Tau is pleased to add: *The University in Process.*

Acknowledgments

I wish to thank the Macmillan Company for permission to quote extensively from Michael St. John Packe, *The Life of John Stuart Mill* (copyright 1954); the Center for Continuing Liberal Education, College of the Liberal Arts, the Pennsylvania State University, for permission to quote a lengthy passage from Bernard J. Muller-Thym's address, "Technological Change and Its Impact *on Men and Organization*," presented at the Conference on Technological Change and Human Values, December 4-6, 1963, sponsored by the Center; the *New England Journal of Medicine* for permission to quote an even lengthier passage from Roscoe Pound's article on "The Professions in the Society of Today"; the Fund for the Advancement of Education for permission to quote two passages from the Donald H. Morison part of Beardsley Ruml's *Memo to a College Trustee;* The Humanities Press, Inc., for permission to quote a lengthy passage from Maurice Merleau-Ponty, *Phenomenology of Perception* (copyright 1962); and the Henry Regnery Company, Publishers, for permission to quote from Gabriel Marcel, *The Mystery of Being* (Gateway Edition, published 1960, all rights reserved).

In justice I acknowledge also a heavy debt to my colleagues Victor Michael Hamm and Kenneth L. Schmitz for their forbearance with my importunate request that they read the earlier drafts of the address, and for their helpfulness both with the drafts and in the choice of a title. I owe the title to the former. I am grateful to both.

I also gratefully acknowledge the care with which my colleague, Francis C. Wade, S.J., prepared the manuscript for publication, and for his helpful suggestions in the process. I thank the Marquette University Press for undertaking the publication.

As a kind of first cause in the sequence of events is the invitation of Wisconsin-Alpha Chapter of the Phi Sigma Tau to present the address. I acknowledge their kindness in extending the invitation, and thank them warmly and in depth for the confidence and the honor which it implies.

The University in Process

The honor implicit in the invitation to give the Aquinas Lecture makes me deeply conscious of the debt I owe my illustrious predecessors on this platform for the grace and dignity with which they have endowed it. The honor you accord me in coming to hear the lecture emphasizes my accountability to you for both my choice of subject and the development of it. I am therefore especially concerned to set at rest any doubts I may have raised about the purpose of my discourse.

I

It must surely seem presumptuous of me to bring to an academic audience a subject in which they have equal claim to competence. As the Germans say, it is like bringing owls to Athens. I disavow that intention. I wish simply to point out some discrepancies which I have found between the historical functions of universities and current practice. The facts are well known to you, and I repeat them only to put them into context. The configuration of the facts, I hope, will give a new insight into some problems of universities in the United States today, and perhaps contribute something to their resolution. I define my purpose, then, as somewhat like the magical rhyme for the bride: that she wear, "something old, something new, something borrowed, something blue." If I exceed the bounds of credibility in what I say, in this my blue period, I hope that you will see it simply as a feature of the hazy borderland between rhyme and magic, or more prosaically, between familiar facts and how one fancies them.

The first context in which I see universities in the United States is in the group of fundamental associations which I have labelled human societies. They include industrial corporations, research foundations, government, churches and professional associations. The feature which unites them is a concern for the social order, for what Thomas More called "the weal public."[1] The people who are the membership of these associations have each his private, individual interest, and they, as does every private citizen, must subordinate that interest to the public good. But members of the associations which I have called human societies have a special responsibility for the structure of the social order. They are architects and builders of it, not simply responsible occupants. The universities belong in this context.

The second context in which I see universities is in the group of arts and crafts. The distinctive art of the universities is that of teaching the skills of the human societies. Implicit in the art is a high regard for learning, and an interest in the uses of learning for the public good.

The discrepancies which I wish to expose as between the historical functions of universities and current practice are principally in the relation of the universities to other human societies. They are three: (1) between the universities as once the sole agency for the advancement of learning and for the teaching of all the useful sciences and their present sharing of that agency with many other human societies; (2) between the universities in the past as almost exclusively educator of clerics and their present function as educator of all but clerics; (3) between the universities as formerly the sole arbiters of professional education and standards and their present function as instruments of professional associations.

The three discrepancies will be indicated hereafter simply by the phrases: the advancement of learning, theology, and the learned professions. They will be considered in that order.

II

The advancement of learning is Francis Bacon's phrase. It probably indicated, in the first Elizabethan age, that people in power should be as much concerned with enlarging the frontier of useful knowledge as they were with enlarging their geographical frontier. The two frontiers were brought together in the Utopian literature.

In *The New Atlantis* (1627) Englishmen discovered an ancient civilization in which learning was institutionalized in a scientific society known as Salomon's House. In the words of the "Father" of the society:

> The End of our Foundation is the knowledge of Causes, and secret motions of things; and the enlarging of the bounds of Human Empire, to the effecting of all things possible.[2]

In the earlier book *Utopia* (1516,) the great discovery was of the marvellous island of that name. The great contribution which Thomas More's narrator, Raphael Hythloday, made on his last visit there, in addition to a knowledge of the Christian religion, was to teach the islanders Greek, out of books he had thoughtfully brought with him, and "the science of imprinting and the craft of making paper,"[3] so that they could efficiently produce numerous copies of the books.

I do not know the source of the notion that the function of a university should be equated with universal knowledge. Samuel Johnson, in his *Dictionary* (1755), defined a university as "a school, where all the arts and faculties are taught and studied." He attributed the definition to "Clarendon,"[4] that is, to Edward Hyde, First Earl of Clarendon, who had been elected chancellor of Oxford University in 1660. John Henry Newman quoted the definition with approval in the first of his discourses at the Catholic University of Dublin in 1852 *On the Scope and Nature of University Education*. He said in amplification:

> As to the range of university teaching, certainly the very name is inconsistent with restrictions of any kind. Whatever was the original reason of its adoption, which is unknown,[5] I am only putting on it its popular, its recognized sense, when I say that a university should teach universal knowledge.[6]

In the hundred years since Newman's discourses the store of men's knowledge has been tremendously expanded. The expansion is measurable in several ways. One of these is volume.

On February 26, 1815, Thomas Jefferson wrote to B. S. Barton requesting return of a book of which he had asked the use some time before. Jefferson stated that,

> Congress having concluded to replace by my library the one they lost by British vandalism, it is now become their property and of course my duty to collect and put in place whatever stood in the catalogue by which they purchased.[7]

The catalogue listed approximately five thousand titles in somewhat more than six thousand volumes.[8] The Library of Congress was moved from the Capitol to a separate building in 1897. The annex was completed in 1939, and is now inadequate for the more than thirty million catalogued items. A rule of thumb for estimating the expansion of a university library is that it doubles its holdings in fourteen years. Such expansion follows a geometrical curve which indicates an increase in the rate of growth as well as in the absolute growth.

Another measure of the expansion in the store of men's knowledge is the number of people engaged as scientists and research workers. I am not in a position to validate the statement that seventy percent of the scientists, who are known to have lived through all recorded history, are alive today. The statement loses some of its dramatic force when seen alongside the estimate that the world's population doubled in the last fifty years, and that a significant percentage of all mankind is alive today. But it does not lose the force of current statistics. A survey made of science manpower in 1962 resulted in a name list of 215,000 scientists in the United States with indicators of the scientific specialization of each.[9]

A third measure of the expansion in the store of men's knowledge is the increase in the number and kind of organizations engaged in research. Research has become an accepted function of industrial corporations, so that some have staffs which are the envy of universities. Several corporations have been formed strictly for research; among them, The Rand Corporation of Santa Monica, and the Hudson Institute at Harmon-on-Hudson.

The governmental interest in research has also increased far beyond military and economic matters. The National Institutes of Health and the National Science Foundation sponsor research at an accelerating rate. The National Space Administration has wide-ranging interests, including human physiology and the botany of food plants.

Many professional associations have their own journals to bring research to the notice of their membership. The *NEA Journal*, started in 1921 by the National Education Association of the United States, the weekly *Journal of the American Medical Association*, *Today's Health* and nine other monthly journals devoted to special fields of medicine, published by the American Medical Association, and the monthly *American Bar Association Journal* are examples. There is also the *Journal of Legal Education*, published quarterly by the Association of American Law Schools. The associations also sponsor research on subjects of interest to them.

One problem for the universities in the current advancement of learning is the volume of it. Exotic languages, area studies, inter-disciplinary sciences and specialized knowledges of many kinds can be maintained with difficulty by each institution. The universities of a region have been forced to divide the less common studies among them, together with the responsibility for building the appropriate library holdings. In this way they have retained the specialties in the region, and kept access to the literature.[10]

Another problem in the advancement of learning is that the universities no longer have a monopoly of research. Their relationship with the other agencies engaged in research must be closer than it was. Their position in the advancement of learning is radically altered, and requires radical modifications of traditional university practice.

III

Theology is the heading of the second discrepancy which we are to discuss. The early colonial colleges were religious foundations. Their support came from churches and their objective was to supply educated ministers of the Gospel. In this they were similar to the mediaeval universities.

In Puritan society all purposes subserved the Christian purpose. It should have been said, therefore, that state, school and church, being alike of human ministry, were alike subservient to the Christian purpose. There was a tendency, however, to see the Christian purpose embodied in one of its instrumentalities. People who saw the state as its embodiment, made church and school subservient to the state. Others who saw the church as its embodiment, made state and school subservient to the church. There may also have been some, though I do not know any, who tried to make the school a similar center of power. I am reminded of the possibility by John Stuart Mill, who in his correspondence with Auguste Comte and to his unconcealed delight, spoke of a pedantocracy.[11]

A difficulty for the universities arose with the adoption of the Constitution of the United States. There was the first article of amendment forbidding Congress to legislate "respecting an establishment of religion, or prohibiting the free exercise thereof." When universities were established by the States the article was invoked. A case in point is that of the University of Virginia.

In the *Report of the Commissioners Appointed to Fix the Site of the University of Virginia &c.*, August 4, 1818, written by Thomas Jefferson, the reasoning and intent are clear. It reads:

> In conformity with the principles of our Constitution, which places all sects of religion on an equal footing, with the jealousies of the different sects in guarding that equality from encroachment and surprise, and with the sentiments of the Legislature in favor of freedom of religion,[12] manifested on former occasions, we have proposed no professor of divinity.[13]

The report, however, made two extenuating provisions. First, the proofs for the existence of "a God, the creator, preserver, and supreme ruler of the universe, the author of all the relations of morality, and of the laws and obligations these infer," were to be within the province of the professor of ethics. Second, instruction in the Hebrew, Greek and Latin languages would be given. The paragraph ends with this sentence:

> Proceeding thus far without offence to the Constitution, we have thought it proper at this point to leave every sect to provide, as they think fittest, the means of further instruction in their own particular tenets.

The University was governed by a Board of Visitors whose elected chairman was called rector. Thomas Jefferson was the first rector. At a meeting of the Visitors, October 7, 1822, at the University, "sectarian schools of divinity" under private sponsorship were permitted "on the confines of the University."[14] At a meeting two years later, on October 4, 1824, the following were among the approved regulations:

> Should the religious sects of this State, or any of them, according to the invitation held out to them, establish within, or adjacent to, the precincts of the University, schools for instruction in the religion of their sect, the students of the University will be free, and expected to attend religious worship at the establishment of their respective sects, in the morning, and in time to meet their school in the University at its stated hour.
>
> The students of such religious school, if they attend any school of the University, shall be considered as students of the University, subject to the same regulations, and entitled to the same rights and privileges.[15]

This resolution of the problem became the precedent in Virginia, and regulations for universities established by many other States took it as their model. Some of the older private universities, perhaps for similar reasons, displaced their faculties of theology from the dominant position they had held, and gave them a peripheral function.

IV

The third discrepancy which we plan to discuss is education for the professions. Having noted the exclusion of theology, and by way of corollary canon law, we have remaining the traditional faculties of civil law, medicine and the liberal arts.

Universities in the United States were slow to establish faculties of medicine. In 1765 the College and Academy of Philadelphia, which later became the University of Pennsylvania, assumed responsibility for the education of physicians. In 1767 a school of medicine was established by King's College which is now Columbia University. The Philadelphia College of Pharmacy, an association of pharmacists, began in 1821 a school for the instruction of pharmacists, as a supplement to apprenticeship.

The first professorship of law was established at the College of William and Mary in 1779. The first law school in the United States was the Litchfield Law School, begun in 1784 by a lawyer, Tapping Reeve, in his private office at Litchfield, Connecticut. The first permanent faculty of law was established by the University of Maryland in 1816. The School of Law at Harvard College was established in 1817. A private law school was adopted by Yale College in 1824.

The plans for the University of Virginia included faculties of medicine, law, architecture, and military science. The phrase Jefferson used frequently in his drafts of the plans was "all the useful sciences." He wanted these taught in their highest degree.[16] Latin, Greek, Hebrew and Anglo-Saxon were in his estimation useful.[17] "The Oriental learning," though formerly esteemed, "may now be omitted," he said.[18]

Alongside what he called "the professional characters," he spoke also of a "civil character,"[19] which was the art of government. He was concerned that there be people who would understand the principles of popular government, as well as the court practices and legislative procedures upon which it rested. To this end the University of Virginia was to give instruction in "the general principles of liberty and the rights of man, in nature and in society," and the distinctive principles of the government of Virginia and of the United States.[20]

The universities of the United States did not develop standards of the professions appropriate to the development of learning in those fields. The tendency both in the United States and in Great Britain was to denigrate professional learning.

John Stuart Mill, whose works were published with his consent in American editions, widely read and admired, said in his inaugural address as rector, delivered to the University of St. Andrews, February 1, 1867:

> The proper function of a University in national education is tolerably well understood. At least there is a tolerably general agreement about what a University is not. It is not a place of professional education. Universities are not intended to teach the knowledge required to fit men for some special mode of gaining their livelihood. Their object is not to make skilful lawyers, or physicians, or engineers, but capable and cultivated human beings.[21]

He said that there should be schools of law and of medicine, and it would be well if there were also schools of engineering and the industrial arts. He saw some advantage in having them in the same localities and under the same general superintendence as "the establishments devoted to education properly so called." He added:

Men are men before they are lawyers, or physicians, or merchants, or manufacturers; and if you make them capable and sensible men, they will make themselves capable and sensible lawyers or physicians. What professional men should carry away with them from a University, is not professional knowledge, but that which should direct the use of their professional knowledge, and bring the light of general culture to illuminate the technicalities of a special pursuit. Men may be competent lawyers without general education, but it depends on general education to make them philosophic lawyers—who demand, and are capable of apprehending, principles, instead of merely cramming their memory with details. And so of all other useful pursuits, mechanical included.[22]

The best known survey of fact regarding education for the professions was made of medical education in the United States and Canada by Abraham Flexner, 1908-1910, under the auspices of the Carnegie Foundation for the Advancement of Teaching.[23] Flexner pointed out the deficiencies in medical education, and attracted attention to the need for better laboratory and clinical facilities and better trained teaching staffs. He inspired the General Education Board, the Rockefeller Foundation and a large number of private donors to contribute to the improvement. The Council on Medical Education and Hospitals, begun in 1904 as a committee of the American Medical Association, provided supervision and control of medical education. Many medical schools were closed, many others consolidated. Medical education in the United States was rapidly and dramatically improved.

The American Bar Association, established in 1878, maintains through its section of Legal Education and Admission to the Bar a list of schools bearing its approval, and an implementing plan of inspection and accreditation.[24] The condition of legal education at the turn of the century was thought to be especially bad because of the long-standing practice of "reading" law with an attorney who had been admitted to the bar, and passing the state bar examination with little or no formal professional schooling. Many schools instructed on a basis of part-time attendance, in the evening, with the primary purpose of preparing their students for the bar examination. The changes made in legal education were not so far-reaching as those in medical. Their effect, however, was similar in that it led to strictly prescribed schooling and, in the 1920's, reform of curriculum and teaching methods.

A third system of accreditation was that of teacher education. Regional bodies, such as the North Central Association of Colleges and Secondary Schools established in 1895, took control over the curriculum and teacher qualifications in the schools of their region.[25] The Association of American Universities, organized in

1900, maintained a list of accredited graduate departments. The American Association of Teachers Colleges, founded in 1917, did the same for institutions preparing teachers. For most functions of education the National Education Association of the United States has been the controlling body, since it received its name and a charter from Congress in 1907.[26]

In a recent realignment of function, the Association of American Universities ceded to the regional bodies the accrediting of graduate departments, and the National Council for Accreditation of Teacher Education since its establishment in 1952 became the accrediting body for programs of teacher education.[27]

In the path of this development there came a long line of other professional associations that took upon themselves the accrediting of the educational programs of their respective professions. The American Council on Pharmaceutical Education (1932), the Engineers' Council for Professional Development (1932), the National Architectural Accrediting Board

(1940), and the Committee on Professional Training of the American Chemical Society (national charter 1938) are examples. The problem became so acute for universities of complex structure that they were forced to appoint staff with the specific function of keeping track of all accreditations, and of preparing for the periodic inspections required to keep them current.

The schools also entered into association. The Association of American Medical Colleges was organized in 1876, the Association of American Law Schools in 1900.

The shift of the center of discretion, and hence of power, from the universities to the professional associations was not a perfect solution. Professional associations have their private objectives which are not entirely expressive of the public interest and the public good, which the professions by their nature and definition are sworn to serve: physicians by the Hippocratic oath, and lawyers by the oath to uphold the Constitution and the laws.[28]

Whereas no satisfactory substitute for self-regulation on the part of a profession with a minimum of direction through state and federal legislation has been found, the professional associations have on occasion let their private interest dictate their action. A frequently cited example is the use of accreditation made by the American Medical Association to limit the number of physicians and surgeons in time of peace to the point of dangerous inadequacy in time of war. The American Bar Association did not act as forcefully to limit enrollment. It had, however, insisted upon a strict case method of instruction, to the neglect of the philosophy of law.

The National Education Association of the United States specified such a concentration in courses on methods of teaching that subject matter was seriously neglected. The inadequacy of teacher preparation was sketched dramatically for the people in the self-survey attendant upon Soviet successes in space science. Through the initiative of private foundations and quasi-governmental agencies a fundamental evaluation was made. The studies of James Bryant Conant, on grants from the Carnegie Corporation of New York,[29] have had far-reaching effects. The success of the National Science Foundation in advancing instruction in mathematics and science has led to programs in The National Defense Education Act of 1958 to upgrade instruction in languages, and to a nation-wide movement for a National Humanities Foundation.

Education for the learned professions is currently under the scrutiny of many agencies. The programs of study in medicine and engineering have become especially unbalanced by the advances in the sciences and technology. The time when professional skills were easily defined and simply acquired by a few who wished them has passed.

V

The recital of discrepancies between past and present has given us an historical perspective for our analysis of the current university situation. Several statements can now be made. The first of these is of university research.

Nathan M. Pusey, president of Harvard University, said that the interest in research came from the German universities, rather than from the British educational practice w h i c h Newman described. Pusey[30] quoted a statement of Friedrich Paulsen (1846-1908), made at the turn of the century, that the teachers of the German universities "were the true exponents of scientific research, and its students the scholars of the future." A description of the research appropriate to universities is in order.

It is not possible to describe it by way of subject matter. There is no longer a recognizable distinction between pure and applied science. The best opinion among scientists is that all new knowledge is important and will some day become meaningful in a larger configuration of facts.

Directors of research in industry cannot easily say what threads of investigation will be profitable. They are willing to risk capital and budget sums of increasing size for research in their conviction that useful contexts of meaning will be discovered. They are not bound by the present line of products. Their companies are accustomed to diversify corporate holdings, and to merge, buy, co-produce, or sell for the sake of balanced growth.

Directors of research in government find it necessary to answer basic questions about the structure of atoms and the chemistry of cells, which in any other age would have been called pure science. The current research interests of government agencies are as much in fundamental science as are those of university laboratories.

It is not possible to describe research appropriate to universities by way of instrumentation or method. Research has become so complex that it requires a team or a larger group to carry it forward.[31] Large and complicated instruments are necessary for some projects, and they require persons with special skills to operate and maintain them. Many and varied competences must be brought together to program the research. Organizing the competences to bring the project to completion has become a major art requiring specialized personnel.

Other research projects are planned for several persons working independently. They too are programmed to reach a specific answer, whether favorable or negative, in a specified time. They require skilled coordinators for all stages of the work.

A new attitude towards invention has developed in the last dozen years.[32] Invention is no longer thought of as a result of accident or good fortune, but as a deliberate process with a precise methodology, so that the planners can set a target date when the objective is to be achieved. Much current research depends upon the invention of new instruments. Research and production have become wedded, so that there is difficulty in distinguishing between them. A university laboratory may thus be as likely a source of a "consumer item" as is an industrial corporation.

Since universities cannot easily determine the kind of research appropriate to them, their judgment in regard to contract research is complicated. Their only stable criterion would seem to be that such research be part of the teaching process, that is, appropriate to the development of young scientists and men of learning.

VI

Another statement that can be made about the current situation of universities refers to potential restraints of their freedom.

Any such restraint would be resisted if it were an obvious use of direct pressure or a deliberate exercise of power. It can, however, happen inadvertently as a result of some program or procedure. Some educators have called attention to the effect of contract research in reshaping university objectives and the large percentage of income which the proceeds of research for government agencies constitute in some university budgets.

Roscoe Pound, former dean of the Harvard Law School, in an address on "The Professions in the Society of Today" which he made to physicians at Worcester in 1949, said:

> Under a system by which local funds for research or for teaching are derived from the national capital even the small part allocated to a locality imposes a kind of censorship on the local authorities. In their eagerness to share in the governmental distribution local officials are loth to make statements or espouse ideas out of conformity with the political or economic doctrines or aims of the central administration or in conflict with the scientific doctrines that its bureaus advocate. Government propaganda goes on upon a large and increasing scale, and dissent is silenced. The effect of this upon a learned art pursued in the spirit of a public service cannot fail to be destructive. How can scientists disagree with the government-promoted doctrines, how can advocates stand up against arbitrary bureaucratic administrative action, how can teachers teach the truth against officially approved doctrines when disagreement means failure to get government grants for research or government subsidies for the institution in which one is employed, or government appointments or assignments to salaried positions?[33]

The nub of the issue is not primarily that government-promoted doctrines tend to quash their opposition, though this occurs, but rather that the simple declaration of government interests and support has the effect of establishing the priorities of fruitful inquiry.

The universities are in a similar way subject to the official views of those professional associations which are also the accrediting bodies. The chief difficulty for professional associations in taking a position on an issue is that their very posture has the undesirable effect of seeming to take the issue out of the forum and to render it no longer debatable. Professional associations can also appear in their posture to threaten reprisal through the application of organized professional power against the expression of a minority opinion.

It is also possible for universities to be under inadvertent restraint of a group that starts with some such statement as, the existence of universities is in the public interest, and concludes that they should agree with the government position on current issues with about the same alacrity as a foreign service officer does the daily guidelines out of Washington. Another example is that of a group that starts with some such statement as, theology is the queen of the sciences, or religious values are highest, and concludes that a university should see to it that theology be part of every other science, and the current level of knowledge in theology the criterion of all other knowledge.

It is possible, too, because a university was founded by some agency of state or church, to conclude to some concept of absolute title and control. A university, no matter how created, must be free to live its proper life. The same is true of the creation of a political society, or a church; no matter how created, they must be free to pursue their purpose. Human societies have a life which is their own, whatever their parentage or condition of birth. The action of founding is simply a midwifery. If some other concept presided over the founding or in subsequent administration, a human society was not born at all, but a monstrous thing with some slight resemblance to what it should have been.

Human societies are autonomous, even as human beings are. It would therefore seem reasonable that the interrelations among autonomous societies would be subject to the same requirements of accommodation as the interrelations among autonomous individuals.

VII

A third statement that can be made about the situation of universities today concerns their teaching function.

It is not immediately evident that their way of teaching is the best way of transmitting knowledge or of extending its frontiers. Industry and government have educational programs on a level comparable to that of universities. Management development programs and the Foreign Service Institute are examples.

Research competences have moved from the universities into many other places. Some industrial corporations still have a tendency to apply the skills of production and sales management to their research divisions, to the discomfort of the scientists. On the other hand, there is a tendency in universities to imitate industrial models of administration. It is hard to predict what the outcome will be. Industry can easily develop a more congenial environment for its research personnel. The day may not be far off when a man who seeks the opportunity for research in projects of his own choice, to be done at his own pace with colleagues congenial to him, may find it the more easily outside the universities. At present, however, there are advantages with the universities. These advantages are clustered around the teaching function.

The universities would seem to have a combination of assets which are most favorable to teaching. The universities do not, or at least need not raise the question of the utility of the knowledge pursued, other than its utility in teaching. The universities traditionally have cherished a respect for learning. They afford the leisure

to at least some people for intensive research experience in apprenticeship with
masters. They afford excellent opportunity
for inter-disciplinary approaches to problems with a maximum possibility of discovering new contexts of meaning. When
they are at their best they are an environment conducive to developing an interest
in learning and in the advancement of it.

If these advantages of the universities as
teaching bodies are admitted, it is possible to describe the relations of the universities to state and church, to professional associations, to industry, and to a
great variety of other research agencies
without threat to the prerogatives of any.
The important point is that all these human societies have become markets for
scientists and other men of learning, and
should therefore out of private interest be
concerned for the welfare of the society
which is the source of the supply. In other
words, it is in the common interest that
the integrity of the universities in their
teaching be preserved and protected.

VIII

The argument to this juncture has been a recital of discrepancies between the historical purposes of universities and their present purposes. The headings for these discrepancies were the advancement of learning, theology, and the secular professions. The historical perspective which the analysis of the discrepancies afforded led to several statements about the current situation of the universities. The headings of these statements were university research, academic freedom, and university teaching. Out of these statements and the historical discrepancies which are their root, it is now possible to make some applications. The first is to a theory of administration.

Administratively universities are subject to the same basic alternatives as other human societies. The most basic of these is the alternative between centralized direction and dispersal of discretionary power and decision.

Max Weber is looked to by some[34] as the classic expositor of centralized control.

Weber described in detail in his *Economics and Society* (1922) two models of it, bureaucratic management and charismatic leadership.[35] He said that the second led to the first, and that the first, bureaucracy, was institutionalized in an office hierarchy and graded authority. In his words,

> The principles of office hierarchy and of levels of graded authority mean a firmly ordered system of super- and subordination in which there is a supervision of the lower offices by the higher ones. Such a system offers the governed the possibility of appealing the decision of a lower office to its highest authority, in a definitely regulated manner. With the full development of the bureaucratic type, the office hierarchy is monocratically organized.[36]

The question is whether such theory of management is appropriate to a university.

The administrative structure of every university, when depicted on an organization chart, gives the impression of having a standard hierarchical pattern, resembling bureaucracy in church, state, the military and industry.[37] It is difficult to tell from the chart what the actual situation is. The similarity of the charts is for some educators a sufficient point of analogy to conclude that the administration of a university should have one of the other human societies as its model. The reasoning is parallel to that of Captain Georg von Trapp in the stage presentation, *The Sound of Music*, who saw nothing incongruous in transferring naval ship's customs and discipline to his household of seven children and their governess. The reasoning, however, is open to several corrections.

Clark Kerr, president of the University of California, has indicated one correction by his use of the term, 'multiversity.' He meant that the functions and structure of a large university are so complex that the traditional term, 'university,' is no longer accurate. He showed that centralized control was more an illusion than a reality.[38]

Donald H. Morison, in a report for The Fund for the Advancement of Education in 1959 has indicated another correction. He stated that the departmental organization is characteristic of colleges and universities in the United States, and is present in them to a greater or lesser degree, "in its most extreme form in large universities."[39] He did not make the statement as a simple recital of fact. He saw the fact as an expression of a fundamental reality. He said:

The departments represent the disciplines in which members of the faculty are trained and by the development of which they obtain their greatest recognition and personal fulfillment. It is normally with departmental colleagues that members of the faculty have most of their working relationships. The department is the mechanism through which professional needs are met and professional standards are enforced. Often it is also the most rewarding social group to which the faculty member belongs. These relationships are recognized and strengthened by the custom of having members of a department housed in adjacent offices in the same building.[40]

Morison drew the conclusion that the "chain of command" is a weak line of influence, and that the departmental chairman is the normal way by which a faculty expresses its opinions, as well as the normal way by which a president or dean influences the faculty.[41] Morison and Kerr have in the effect of their statements, pointed in the same direction.

The important point in the argument for dispersal of discretion, therefore, is that decisions should be made by people who have the knowledge appropriate to the decisions. In the present type of university organization in the United States, the place of decision would normally, but not exclusively, be the department. Exceptions would be other quasi-departmental structures, such as institutes, programs, or other teaching groups.

The teaching aspect remains paramount, partly because it is the distinctive feature of a university, and partly because it is the locus of power. A university is characteristically what its faculties are. Its faculties do the teaching, and are the continuity of the institution. The vital decisions of a university are those that select the faculties. These decisions are made normally by the present faculties, in whatever groupings the expert knowledge appropriate to each decision can best be identified and marshalled. An extraordinary situation is, for example, one in which an entirely new area of competence is under development, or one in which the present faculty has shown itself unable or unwilling to make the appropriate decision. Normally the senior members of a department are recognized as having the expert knowledge and competence to make the best decisions regarding selection, tenure and advancement of the faculty. A department that consistently fails to attract good faculty spends a correspondingly large part of its resources on the apology for its existence.[42]

The contribution which the presidents of some universities have made to the development of outstanding faculties is also part of history. Among the notable examples are Daniel Coit Gilman (1831-1908) in the development of The Johns Hopkins University,[43] William Rainey Harper (1856-1906) as first president of the University of Chicago, and more recently, Herman B. Wells (1902-   ), of Indiana

University.[44] The achievement of Abraham Flexner (1866-1959) as director of the Institute for Advanced Study at Princeton, 1930 to 1939, is also worthy of record. The common element in the stories of their accomplishment is that they made the development of their faculties a matter of personal concern and highest priority, and their estimation of the matter was known throughout their institution.

There are decisions, however, that are not simply ones of obtaining and retaining the most competent teachers in an area of knowledge. Budget limitations put departments into competition for available funds. Eric Ashby, master of Clare College, Cambridge University, said: "In any healthy institution innovation and enthusiasm outrun resources and so there arises a succession of conflicts."[45] Decisions regarding such conflicts are arbitrated, so that the faculties are convinced that the best interests of the university are served. Such decisions are especially delicate when some areas are selected for expansion. A second important contribution of the president is to negotiate these and all other cases of competition or dispute among faculties, and to work to create the necessary cohesion in the faculties.

As in matters of the political order, so in universities, it is less a point of concern how the president comes to be named to the position, than it is how he acts in office. Presidents who consistently act contrary to what in the opinion of the faculties is in the best interest of the university, or habitually fail to act, will set into motion ingenious and varied tactical maneuvers,[46] not only within the university and in other universities, but also in the other human societies to which the university is related. Good teachers may leave, recruitment of replacements may be difficult and more expensive, financial support may lag and the community in which the university is situated may lose interest. The best asset that a university president can have is the confidence of a competent faculty.

The perpetuation of an institution is an especially delicate operation. Some industrial companies have done remarkably well for generations. Religious and charitable societies have also succeeded. An outstanding example of success is that of the old private universities whose boards of governors have for centuries kept them legally in being, financially solvent, and academically superior. Many such boards are self-perpetuating, the present membership being the final, if not the sole body to fill its vacancies. Their success has not been without periods of trouble and controversy. It has required the resources and competences of dedicated men who had a clear understanding of the task. They can have applied to them what Alfred North Whitehead said of the universities: "By their agency the adventure of action met the adventure of thought."[47]

IX

The second application of the discrepancies noted earlier, and the statements derived from them, is to a theory of creativity.

Some aspects of the subject are obvious. Universities properly make the creative arts objects of concern. Creative writing is a recognized responsibility of departments of literature. Scientists are at their best when they are creative. All research should have nodding acquaintance with creativity. Less obvious is the proposition that teaching is not truly teaching, and learning is not learning, unless it is creative. A corollary is that teaching which is not creative contributes nothing to the end of learning. The proposition and its corollary are worthy of our attention.

Knowledge has excited the wonder and curiosity of men since Pythagoras described himself as a lover of wisdom. The mystery of it has caused men to see in it the vestiges of the divine and to point to the lost pillars of Hermes and their inscriptions, which both Pythagoras and Plato read at Thebes,[48] as monumental evidence of the concourse which men had had with the god.

The imparting of knowledge shares in the mystery of all knowledge, and adds to it the parameter of the concourse of men with their fellows.

It has been observed that knowledge does not keep well in books. If it did, the phenomenon which Marshall McLuhan called "the Gutenberg galaxy"[49] would not exist. His studies showed the influence of the medium of communication on the message. They pointed to knowledge as a living activity textured by the context of its imparting.

Whitehead's remark was that,

Knowledge does not keep any better than fish. You may be dealing with knowledge of the old species, with some old truth; but somehow or other it must come to the students, as it were, just drawn out of the sea and with the freshness of its immediate importance.[50]

Another evidence of the mystery of knowledge is that teachers are necessary for students who wish to learn, and students are necessary for teachers who wish to advance learning. It would seem that the reverse should be true, namely that the only important element in learning is students, and the only important element in the advancement of learning is teachers. And indeed there are times when students feel that teachers stand in the way of learning, and times when teachers feel that learning would be advanced at an accelerated rate if there were no students. The experience of the race is a rejection of this feeling.

The most advanced technology of communication has not appreciably changed the ancient relationship of teacher and student. Closed circuit television with built-in "feedback," used extensively in the earlier years of college, has simply accentuated the need for the closest apprenticeship in the years of specialization and graduate study. The same phenomenon has occurred in the theatre. The development of television theatre has as its concomitant a legitimate theatre more intimately "in-the-round," with more direct audience participation, than any previous theatre.

A similar phenomenon occurs among research workers. What would seem to be an advantage to work without the interruptions from students, ends with a yearning for the stimulus of their presence, and a need to return to teaching for the sake of the research.

Explanations for these two phenomena have been sought in many areas. A sociological explanation points to the gregariousness of men. An anthropological explanation emphasizes the transmission of the skills of survival as essential to the continuance of the race. A psychological explanation sees in youth the vivid imagination and mimicry necessary for the acquisition of knowledge. Each of these explanations is little more than an elaborated statement of the mystery, which for all the explanation remains a mystery.

All learning is creative. The learner must create each segment of knowledge, either poetically as one does one's fancies, or architectonically as one does one's purposes. There are no simple facts, as if they could exist apart from imagining or making. And facts are not got except through the search which is the motor of invention and discovery.

A teacher qualified for this kind of learning situation has the ability to set the search in motion.[51] He offers students the opportunity of discovery and invention. John Dewey had this in mind when he argued for learning by doing.[52] His formula was open to quite as much abuse as the older formulae. A pedantic teacher can make a series of laboratory experiments as meaningless a routine as he can a book, instead of the exciting rediscovery which both were intended to be.

The question is what keeps a teacher imaginative. Part of the secret is probably a teacher's exposure to the concerns of students about themselves and their age, and the pretty fardel of suspicions which they bring with them to the universities. Another part of the secret may be the opportunity for a teacher through research to retain a spirit of invention and discovery. A third factor may be the freedom which a teacher has to propose his ideas tentatively without the harassing worry of public criticism or the responsibility for immediate action.

These are all factors of what biologists call the ecology, and lead to a question about the environment of a teacher in a university.

X

A third application of the material thus far presented is, therefore, to a theory of colleagueship.

I have the term from David Riesman. He used it in an address in April 1958 at Wayne State University as part of a symposium on The College Teacher.[53] He said that he owes his awareness of the problem and his understanding of it to Everett C. Hughes, of the Sociology Department of the University of Chicago.[54]

Riesman described the college teacher's problem of discovering the people who are close to his way of thinking and feeling, and in whose company he can grow and develop. He said that a teacher's true colleagues may be in departments other than his own, and they may change as a teacher's ideas change, so that he "has to guard against too readily continuing membership in any one fraternity, no matter how pleasant and reassuring the company."[55]

The situation can be expressed in philosophical terms. Ancient philosophers have stated that the society of a man's fellows is important to him for the sake of his intellectual development as well as for reasons of friendship. Modern philosophers have applied the proposition to a theory of language, and have stated that language is the way in which a person can attain to being. Maurice Merleau-Ponty said:

> In the experience of dialogue, there is constituted between the other person and myself a common ground; my thoughts and his are interwoven into a single fabric, my words and those of my interlocutor are called forth by the state of the discussion, and they are inserted into a shared operation of which neither of us is the creator. We have here a dual being, where the other is for me no longer a mere bit of behaviour in my transcendental field, nor I in his; we are collaborators for each other in consummate reciprocity. Our perspectives merge into each other, and we co-exist through a common world.[56]

The common world of colleagues has a sufficient justification in the opportunities it affords its membership for personal development. It has another effect, and incidentally further justification, in what might be described as a corporate development.

When many experts are concentrated in what we shall call a "talking distance" of one another, they develop sets of conclusions which have a corporate presence and authority. They develop some of them gradually and unintentionally, not as idols of tribe or marketplace like those which Francis Bacon identified, but as an authentic body of discriminate thought which they share. They are experts by right of their own competence, but they are also recognized for a corporate competence.

The corporate competence has several distinguishing marks. It is *residual*, the result of much concern about many things, yet none of them, nor the sum of them. It is to the group what liberal education is to the individual and what culture and civilization are to society. It is *pervasive* in that its possessors bring it to each practical situation and each decision, just as a learned man brings all his learning, taste and skill to each problem. It is *poetic*, because it is an attitude, an "atmosphere," a harmony, a "morale," in which the specified configuration of a current action takes place. It is also *architectonic*, in the sense of a set of prearranged judgments in the context of which decisions are composed. It is "objectives," "esprit de corps," "principles," "traditions."

The distinguishing marks of the corporate competence indicate that it is a work of time, and "cannot be extemporized to meet an emergency."[57] It is, however, available in an emergency, and can be brought to function in crisis, with minimum delay and maximum effect.

Michael Polanyi, in a lecture delivered at Roosevelt University in January 1962, used the expression "the republic of science."[58] He said:

> The Republic of Science shows us an association of independent initiatives, combined towards an indeterminate achievement. It is disciplined and motivated by serving a traditional authority, but this au-

thority is dynamic; its continued existence depends on its constant self-renewal through the originality of its followers.[59]

Polanyi also applied to it the term, "Society of Explorers," and the concept of self-improvement. He was concerned with the mutual adjustment which independent initiatives require, lest it refuse "the right to opposition in the name of truth." It must leave the situation open-ended so that men of genius have room to emerge.

Isaiah Berlin, in an appraisal of Chaim Weizmann, spoke in general about the phenomenon of a great man. He said:

> The transformation he effects, if he is truly to deserve his title, must be such as those best qualified to judge consider to be antecedently improbable—something unlikely to be brought about by the mere force of events, by the 'trends' or 'tendencies' already working at the time—that is to say, something unlikely to occur without the intervention, difficult or impossible to discount in advance, of the man who for this very reason deserves to be described as great.[60]

Clark Kerr supplied another trenchant concept, that of "Ideopolis" or, "the city of intellect,"[61] in extension of Jacques Barzun's "house of intellect."[62] Kerr was primarily interested in the fact that university centers have a tendency to coalesce and to have clustering around them "scientifically oriented industrial and governmental enterprises." He observed the acceleration of the opportunities of choice which individuals in a metropolis enjoyed.[63] He expressed the hope that the new ideopolis would have a similar power of attraction, and presumably afford to individuals a similar constellation of choices.

Gabriel Marcel said:

> Ought we not to recur here to one of the deepest notions of the Californian philosopher, Josiah Royce,[64] and to say that the man who is engaged in the search for truth enters into an ideal community? He becomes a citizen of a city that is not built with stones and that is cemented only with thought. . . .
>
> The best image, indeed, that we can here evoke that city by, is the simple one of a

discussion about ideas in which both the conversationalists are so interested in their topic that each forgets about himself, which is to say, really, about the personal impression he is making on the other; for the tiniest touch of self-complacency would lower the tone of the discussion. The very soul of such discussions is the joy of communicating, not necessarily the joy of finding that one's views agree with another's; and this distinction between communicating and agreement has great importance.[65]

Through his image of a dialogue Marcel has indicated two aspects of the community of thought. He showed the joy of living in it. He also showed the demands which such life makes on a person. His words were that a person "forgets about himself," avoids "the tiniest touch of self-complacency," and concentrates on "communicating," not on finding "agreement." In these three points Marcel has listed the chief dangers to the community of thought, with much the same sensitivity as the authors of *The Federalist* papers[66] pointed out "the characteristic dangers of popular government." Self-interest, self-complacency, and intolerance of another's views are the dangers which Marcel saw. He summarized them with a question:

> But is it not against this city that the scientist is committing a treason when, out of fear or out of self-interest, he recants the conclusions that he reached in the days when he served truth loyally?"[67]

As in the political order, so in the community of thought, dangers are avoided by knowing them and by setting purpose against them.

XI

The three applications which we have made to educational theory were under the headings of administration, creativity and colleagueship. They were not the only ones that we could make. The justification of their selection is that they are basic, and that they point to fluid aspects of the current situation of the universities. They are, therefore, points of potential impact, where the future of the universities will be decided. Taken in concert they give a preview of what the future might be.

The first noteworthy item of the preview is that the universities will continue in existence. It is an extension to another century of an observation made by David Starr Jordan at the turn of our century. He said, "the true American University lies in the future."[68] He was in no worse position to estimate the situation of today, than we are to estimate for the year 2000.

The second item of the preview is the administrative task. It is the vision of universities in which the chief worry of administrative officials is to attract outstanding faculties and to facilitate their work of teaching and advancing knowledge.

The third item is a sense of expectancy regarding creativity, as if mankind were about to enter a new springtime of hope and accomplishment, far beyond the measure of current imagining. Observers now speak confidently of an impending "cultural explosion." Creativity has been called the most important single element of our culture.[69] In our vision of the universities, creativity will mark both their teaching and their advancement of learning.

Fourth and last on the list of items in our preview is the atmosphere of thought and learning in which universities prosper. It is seen as a construct of cooperative effort and a focus of the genius, ingenuity and wisdom of the age. It induces a vision of a city of intellect, in the midst of the people, and at their disposal for the political good and for the fashioning of a truly social order. It is a vision of the universities of Utopia.[70]

NOTES

1. *Utopia,* in the translation of Ralph Robinson, with introduction and notes by H. B. Cotterill (London: Macmillan and Co., 1928), pp. 19, 20, 22, etc.

2. *The New Atlantis,* ed. J. Spedding, R. L. Ellis, and D. D. Heath, *The Works of Francis Bacon,* 15 volumes (Boston: Houghton, Mifflin and Company, 190-?), V, 398.

3. *Utopia,* book II, chapter vi. Edition cited, p. 108. Both crafts were comparatively recent inventions in Europe. More was evidently unwilling or unable to concede that they could have been invented previously even by the Utopians.

 Shortly before the statement about the crafts More recorded Raphael Hythloday's account of the books: "They have of me (for when I was determined to enter into my fourth voyage, I cast into the ship in the stead of merchandise a pretty fardel of books, because I intended to come again rather never than shortly) they have, I say, of me the most part of Plato's works, more of Aristotle's, also Theophrastus of plants, but in divers places (which I am sorry for) imperfect. For whilst we were a shipboard, a marmoset chanced upon the book, as it was negligently laid by, which wantonly playing therewith plucked out certain leaves and tore them in pieces. Of them that have written the grammar, they have only Lascaris. For Theodorus I carried not with me, nor never a dictionary but Hesychius, and Dioscorides. They set great store by Plutarch's books. And they be delighted with Lucian's merry conceits and jests. Of the poets they have Aristophanes, Homer, Euripides, and Sophocles in Aldus' small print. Of the historians they have Thucydides, Herodotus, and Herodian. Also my companion Tricius Apinatus carried with him physic books, certain small works of Hippocrates and Galen's Microtechne; the which book they have in great estimation." Edition cited, pp. 106-107.

4. *A Dictionary of the English Language,* third edition carefully revised, abstracted from the Folio Edition by the Author (Dublin: Thomas Ewing, 1768) *s.v.* "University." The definition is without attribution in the folio edition (London: W. Strahan, 1755), II, signature 29R.

5. Newman's note: "In Roman law it means a corporation. *Vide* Keuffel, *de Scholis.*"

6. Edition in Everyman's Library (New York: E. P. Dutton & Co., 1915), p. 9. Introduction by Wilfrid Ward.

7. *The Writings of Thomas Jefferson,* 20 volumes (Washington: The Thomas Jefferson Memorial Association, 1905), XIX, 223. See also his letter to Samuel H. Smith, Esq., dated at Monticello, September 21, 1814, describing his library. *The Writings of Thomas Jefferson,* XIV, 190-194.

8. A holograph catalogue begun by Jefferson in 1783 survives. There is also the *Catalogue of the Library of the United States,* prepared

by George Watterston, the newly appointed librarian of Congress, and printed for Congress by Jonathan Eliot at Washington in November 1815. For illustrations and description see E. Millicent Sowerby, compiler, *Catalogue of the Library of Thomas Jefferson,* 5 volumes (Washington: The Library of Congress, 1952-1959), I, after p. [xv]; V, 215-218. A fire in the Capitol, where the books were housed, on Christmas Eve 1851, destroyed an estimated two-thirds of Jefferson's library.

9.   *American Science Manpower 1962, A Report of the National Register of Scientific and Technical Personnel* (Washington: U.S. Government Printing Office, 1964), 155 pp.

10.   See, for example, Redding S. Sugg, Jr., and George Hilton Jones, *The Southern Regional Education Board: Ten Years of Regional Cooperation in Higher Education* (Baton Rouge: Louisiana State University Press, 1960), 179 pp.

11.   Lettre à A. Comte, 25 February, 1842: "Il ne pourrait en résulter que ce qu'on voit dans la Chine, c'est-a-dire une pédantocratie"; Letter to Mill, 4 March 1842: "votre heureuse expression de pédantocratie". Lucien Lévy-Bruhl, *Lettres inédites de John Stuart Mill à Auguste Comte, publiées avec les réponses de Comte et une introduction* (Paris: F. Alcan, 1899), pp. 28, 35. Mill used the English form in *Liberty* (1859), chap. V, near end: "if we would not have our bureaucracy degenerate into a pedantocracy. . . ." (London: Longmans, Green, and Co., 1867), p. 67a.

Michael St. John Packe, in *The Life of John Stuart Mill*, with a preface by F. A. Hayek (New York: The Macmillan Company, 1954), pp. 275-276, says:

"Mill strongly approved of all that Comte had said about the necessity for moral and mental improvement to precede the regeneration of society, and even approved the idea of promulgating a set of sociological maxims, which should have the emotional force of a religion. He agreed that in social as in scientific matters, the general public must accept the guidance of experts who were more 'positivized' than they themselves could hope to be; and that these experts should comprise a sort of philosophic priesthood, with advisory powers sharply distinguished from the powers of government, like the division between the temporal and spiritual powers in the Middle Ages. He even coined the name 'Pedantocracy' for this body, which much delighted Comte."

12. "An Act for establishing Religious Freedom, passed in the Assembly of Virginia in the beginning of the year 1786." It was written by Jefferson. *The Writings of Thomas Jefferson*, II, 300-303.

13. The *Report* is not in *The Writings of Thomas Jefferson*. It is contained in *Early History of the University of Virginia, as Contained in the Letters of Thomas Jefferson and Joseph C. Cabell* (Richmond: John William Randolph, 1856), pp. 432-447; Charles Flinn Arrowood, *Thomas Jefferson and Education in a Republic* (New York: McGraw-Hill Book

Company, 1930), pp. 132-159, last part of the report, about two pages, omitted; Roy J. Honeywell, *The Educational Work of Thomas Jefferson* (Cambridge, Mass.: Harvard University Press, 1931), pp. 248-260.

14. *The Writings of Thomas Jefferson*, XIX, 449.

15. *Ibid.*, XIX, 414-416.

16. Letter to John Adams, dated at Monticello, July 5, 1814, *ibid.*, XIV, 151; letter to Dr. Thomas Cooper, dated at Monticello, August 25, 1814, *ibid.*, XIV, 173; letter to Monsieur A. Coray, dated at Monticello, October 31, 1823, *ibid.*, XV, 487-488.

17. Th. Jefferson, Rector: Report "To the president and directors of the Literary Fund," October 5, 1824, *ibid.*, XIX, 455.

18. Letter to Joseph Priestly, dated at Philadelphia, January 18, 1800, *ibid.*, X, 140-141.

19. Th. Jefferson, Rector: Minutes "At a meeting of the Visitors of the University of Virginia at the said University, on Monday, the 7th of October, 1822," *ibid.*, XIX, 415.

20. Th. Jefferson, Rector: Minutes "'At a special meeting of the Board of Visitors of the University . . . held at the University March 4, 1825," *ibid,.* XIX, 460-461.

21. *Dissertations and Discussions*, 5 volumes (New York: Henry Holt and Company, 1864-1875), IV (1874), 334; *Inaugural Address delivered to the University of St. Andrews*

February 1st 1867 (London: Longmans, Green, and Co., 1897), p. 4.

22. *Dissertations and Discussions*, IV, 335; *Inaugural Address*, pp. 4-5.

23. Published as "Bulletin Number Four" of the Carnegie Foundation for the Advancement of Teaching under the title, *Medical Education in the United States and Canada* (New York, 1910), 346 pp. See also *Abraham Flexner: An Autobiography* (New York: Simon and Schuster, 1960), pp. 70-88. The book is a revision, brought up to date, of Flexner's *I Remember*, published in 1940. Flexner died in 1959 at the age of ninety-two.

See also C. Sidney Burwell, "Some Responsibilities of Medical Education," Annual Oration, presented at the annual meeting of The Massachusetts Medical Society, Worcester, May 24, 1949, *The New England Journal of Medicine*, CCXL (June 9, 1949), 905-910; Walter S. Wiggins and staff, "Medical Education in the United States," the 64th Annual Report of the Council on Medical Education, *The Journal of the American Medical Association*, CXC (November 16, 1964), 597-676; "Editorials," *ibid.*, 677-680; Thomas B. Turner, "The Future of Medicine," in his *Fundamentals of Medical Education* (Springfield, Ill.: Charles C. Thomas, 1963), pp. 73-78.

24. Walter Gellhorn, "The Second and Third Years of Law Study," *Journal of Legal Education*, XVII (1964), 1-15; Karl N. Llewellyn, chairman, Committee on Curriculum, Associ-

ation of American Law Schools, "The Place of Skills in Legal Education," *Columbia Law Review,* XLV (1945), 345-391; Erwin Griswold, "Some Thoughts about Legal Education Today," in *Frontiers in Law and Legal Education* (Ann Arbor, Michigan: University of Michigan Law School, 1961), pp. 75-86; Karl N. Llewellyn, "The Study of Law as a Liberal Art," Address at the Dedicatory Celebrations, University of Chicago Law School, April 30, 1960, in Llewellyn's *Jurisprudence, Realism in Theory and Practice* (Chicago: The University of Chicago Press, 1962), pp. 375-394.

25. See Calvin Olin Davis, *A History of the North Central Association of Colleges and Secondary Schools, 1895-1945* (Ann Arbor, Michigan: The North Central Association of Colleges and Secondary Schools, 1945), 286 pp.

26. Its predecessors were the National Teachers' Association organized at Philadelphia in 1857, and the National Educational Association, a federation of teachers, administrators and normal schools, formed in 1870. See Edgar B. Wesley, *NEA: The First Hundred Years, The Building of the Teaching Profession* (New York: Harper & Brothers, 1957), 419 pp.

27. For a discussion of the complex interrelations of these organizations, see James Bryant Conant, *The Education of American Teachers* (New York: McGraw-Hill Book Company, 1963), pp. 15-22.

28. For a survey of current uses, see Louis Lasagna, "Would Hippocrates Rewrite His Oath?", *The New York Times Magazine,* June 28, 1964, pp. 11, 40-43. See "The Chicago Lawyer's Pledge," in Llewellyn, *Jurisprudence, Realism in Theory and Practice,* cited above, p. 395.

29. *The Education of American Teachers,* 275 pp.; *The American High School Today* (New York: McGraw-Hill Book Company, 1959), 140 pp. For a criticism, see Paul Goodman, *The Community of Scholars* (New York: Random House, 1962), pp. 52-61.

30. "The American University 1960," in his *The Age of the Scholar, Observations on Education in a Troubled Decade* (Cambridge, Massachusetts: The Belknap Press of Harvard University Press, 1963), p. 161.

31. Derek J. De Solla Price, *Little Science, Big Science* (New York: Columbia University Press, 1963), pp. 78-91; William Kornhauser, *Scientists in Industry, Conflict and Accommodation* (Berkeley: University of California Press, 1962), pp. 50-56; Simon Marcson, *The Scientist in American Industry* (New York: Harper & Brothers, 1960), pp. 86-97; Margaret Barron Luszki, *Interdisciplinary Team Research Methods and Problems* (Washington: National Training Laboratories, National Education Association of the United States, 1958), pp. 107-136.

For a view of the related problem of organizational structures, see Robert Presthus, *The Organizational Society, an Analysis and a Theory* (New York: Alfred A. Knopf, 1962), 340 pp.

32. Bernard J. Muller-Thym, "Technological Change and its Impact on Men and Organization," an address given at a Conference on Technological Change and Human Values, the Pennslyvania State University, December 4-6, 1963, p. 3.

"In addition to the recent impact of technology and concurrent collapse of boundaries between various fields of knowledge, there has been a second major development during the past decade: we have invented the organization of invention. Today, when we want to invent something, instead of leaving the process of invention to the chance that nature has provided an Icarus, or a Daedalus or a Leonardo or a Watt or an Eli Whitney, we now deliberately set out to invent things. The process of invention, then, works backwards. We decide what we are going to invent and then, in relation to this, decide what are the competences we need in order to bring this thing into existence. We have invented the manner to mobilize these competences."

On changes caused by technological advances, see Eli Ginzberg, editor, *Technology and Social Change* (New York: Columbia University Press, 1964), 158 pp.; Francis Bello, Mario G. Salvadori and Donald Michael, "The Impact of Science and Technology," in *The Environment of Change*, a Conference at Sterling Forest, Tuxedo, New York, June 14-17, 1964, pp. 9-40.

33.   Presented at the annual meeting of The Massachusetts Medical Society, Worcester, May 25, 1949. *The New England Journal of Medicine*, CCXLI (September 8, 1949), 351-357. I am indebted to Dr. Herbert Ratner, Director of Public Health, Oak Park, Illinois, for the reference. The quotation is from page 356.

34.   Arthur M. Schlesinger, Jr., "On Heroic Leadership" (1960) in his *The Politics of Hope* (Boston: Houghton Mifflin Company, 1962), pp. 9-13; John D. Millett, *The Academic Community, an Essay on Organization* (New York: McGraw-Hill Book Company, 1962), pp. 8, 23-32.

35.   The term "charismatic" has been used for centuries in theology. Its use in the present context, Weber said, was derived from Rudolf Sohm, church historian and jurist at the University of Strassburg. The idea is found in Thomas Carlyle, *Heroes and Hero-Worship* (1841), in Ralph Waldo Emerson's response, *Representative Men* (1850), and in William E. H. Lecky, *History of the Rise and Influence of the Spirit of Rationalism in Europe*, 2 volumes (New York: D. Appleton and Company, 1867), I, 310. See also Lord Raglan (Fitzroy Richard Somerset, 4th Baron Raglan), *The Hero, a Study in Tradition, Myth, and Drama* (New York: Vintage Books, 1956), 308 pp.

36.   *Wirtschaft und Gesellschaft* (Tübingen: J. C. B. Mohr, 1922), part III, chapter 6, p. 650. English translation by H. H. Gerth and

C. Wright Mills, *From Max Weber: Essays in Sociology* (New York: Oxford University Press, 1958), p. 197; in the translation of A. M. Henderson and Talcott Parsons, *Max Weber: The Theory of Social and Economic Organization* (New York: Oxford University Press, 1947), p. 331.

37. Edward H. Litchfield, "Notes on a General Theory of Administration," *Administrative Science Quarterly*, I (June 1956), 28, said: "FIFTH MAJOR PROPOSITION: *Administration and the administrative process occur in substantially the same generalized form in industrial, commercial, civil, educational, military, and hospital organizations.*" See also Herbert Solow, "All-purpose Executive," *Fortune*, LVIII (December 1958), 122-124, 190, 193.

Two analyses of administration are especially helpful: Wilfrid Brown, *Some Problems of a Factory, an Analysis of Industrial Institutions* (London: Institute of Personnel Management, 1952), 20 pp.; Cyril O'Donnell, "The Source of Managerial Authority," *Political Science Quarterly*, LXVII (December 1952), 573-588. On university administration, see John J. Corson, *Governance of Colleges and Universities* (New York: McGraw-Hill Book Company, 1960), pp. 118-142.

38. Clark Kerr, *The Uses of the University* (Cambridge, Massachusetts: Harvard University Press, 1963), pp. 1-45. See also his article, "The Frantic Race to Remain Contemporary," *Daedalus*, XCIII (Fall 1964), 1051-1070; it is adapted in substantial part from *The Uses of the University.*

39. "Achievement of the Possible," in Beardsley Ruml, *Memo to a College Trustee* (New York: McGraw-Hill Book Company, 1959), p. 52.

40. *Ibid.*

41. *Ibid.*, p. 56. In this connection it is interesting to note Thomas Jefferson's opinion about the office of president of a university, which he expressed shortly before his death.

The Board of Visitors of the University of Virginia, meeting at the University on April 3-4, 1826, had voted to establish the office of president. The reason for the action was to secure the services of William Wirt (1772-1834), Attorney-General of the United States, as professor of law and president. If Mr. Wirt declined the appointment, the resolution establishing the office of president would be null and void. Jefferson wrote a dissent, giving four reasons, of which the second was:

"2. Because he is of opinion that every function ascribed to the president by this enactment, can be performed by the faculty, as now established by law." (*The Writings of Thomas Jefferson*, XIX, 493).

Mr. Wirt declined the appointment. The next meeting of the Visitors was held on October 2, 1826, to fill the vacancy in the office of rector caused by the death of Thomas Jefferson. *Ibid.*, XIX, 499.

It was not intended that the University of Virginia have a president. The executive officer was a chairman, elected by the faculty of professors from their own number. The regulation, enacted "at a meeting of the Visitors of the University, on Monday the 4th of October, 1824," was:

"At a meeting of the faculty of professors, on matters within their functions, one of them shall preside, by rotation, for the term of one year each. A majority of the members shall make a quorum for business. They may appoint a secretary of their own body, or otherwise, who shall keep a journal of their proceedings, and lay the same before the Board of Visitors at their first ensuing meeting, and whenever else required. The compensation for such secretary shall be fifty dollars yearly, payable from the funds of the University.

"Meetings of the faculty may be called by the presiding member of the year, or by any three of the professors, to be held in an apartment of the rotunda, and the object of the call shall be expressed in the written notification to be served by the janitor. But when assembled, other business also may be transacted.

"The faculty may appoint a janitor, who shall attend its meetings, and the meetings of the Visitors, and shall perform necessary menial offices for them, for which he shall receive 150 dollars yearly from the funds of the University, and be furnished with a lodging room." *Ibid.*, XIX, 441-442.

42. Karl Jaspers, *The Idea of the University*, in the translation of H. A. T. Reiche and H. F. Vanderschmidt (Boston: The Beacon Press, 1959), p. 71, said:
"Not only the university but all corporate bodies tend to maintain an unconscious solidarity against both the excellent and the

mediocre, prompted by such anti-intellectual motivations as fear of competition and jealousy. The excellent are instinctively excluded from fear of competition, just as the inferior are rejected out of concern for the prestige and influence of the university. The 'competent,' the second-rate, are selected, people who are on the same intellectual level as oneself."

Robert M. Hutchins, "Education and Independent Thought" (February 20, 1952), in his *Freedom, Education, and the Fund: Essays and Addresses, 1946-1956* (New York: Meridian Books, 1956), p. 161, said:

"I do not claim that professors are the only people who can think or the only people who do. I merely say that unless a man can and will think he should not be a professor, and that professors are the only people in the world whose sole duty is to think. To require them to stop thinking, or to think like everybody else, is to defeat the purpose of their lives and of their institution." See also Harold W. Dodds, *The Academic President—Educator or Caretaker?* (New York: McGraw-Hill Book Company, 1962), pp. 124-162: "Building Faculty Personnel."

43. Henry James (1879-1947), *Charles W. Eliot, President of Harvard University, 1869-1909,* 2 volumes (Boston: Houghton Mifflin Company, 1930), II, 17-18, said: "Gilman, however, appeared to be inspired by the belief that when a university proposes to advance knowledge as well as to teach, it is better for it to lay aside the question, What use can be made of the result of investigation? . . .

Gilman was the first American university president to act boldly on the theory and also the first to have an opportunity to practice it with the aid of large resources." See also Francesco Cordasco, *Daniel Coit Gilman and the Protean Ph.D.* (Leiden: E. J. Brill, 1960), 160 pp.

44. William Rainey Harper, "The College President," written in 1904 and first published in *The William Rainey Harper Memorial Conference* (Chicago: The University of Chicago Press, 1938), pp. 25-34; reprinted in part in Edgar W. Knight, *What College Presidents Say* (Chapel Hill, North Carolina: The University of North Carolina Press, 1940), pp. 7-10. See also Thomas Wakefield Goodspeed, *William Rainey Harper, First President of the University of Chicago* (Chicago: The University of Chicago Press, 1928), 241 pp.

Herman B. Wells, "How to Succeed as a University President Without Really Trying," *The Educational Record*, XLV (Summer 1964), 241-245.

45. "A University Presidency: What it Takes," *Saturday Review*, November 21, 1964, p. 77. See also his article, "The Administrator: Bottleneck or Pump?", *Daedalus*, XCI (Spring 1962), pp. 264-278.

46. Donald H. Morison, "Achievement of the Possible," p. 56: "When matters of staffing, of curriculum and of teaching methods are involved, a department's capabilities for resistance are almost unlimited." For a political parallel, see Bertrand de Jouvenel, "The Team

Against the Committee," *The Review of Politics,* XXV (1963), 147-156.

47. "Universities and their Function," an address at the Business School of Harvard University, 1928, *The Atlantic Monthly,* CXLI (May 1928), 638-644; the quotation is from p. 640b. The address was included in Whitehead's *The Aims of Education and other Essays* (New York: The Macmillan Company, 1929), pp. 136-152; the quotation is from p. 143.

48. Iamblichus, "The Answer of the Preceptor Abammon to the Epistle of Porphyry to Anebo, and a Solution of the Doubts contained in it," chapter II, in Thomas Taylor, translator, *Iamblichus on the Mysteries of the Egyptians, Chaldeans, and Assyrians,* second edition (London: Bertram Dobell, 1895), p. 21: "If also you should propose any philosophic inquiry, we shall discuss it for you, according to the ancient pillars of Hermes, which Plato and Pythagoras knew before, and from thence constituted their philosophy."

49. *The Gutenberg Galaxy, the Making of Typographic Man* (Toronto: University of Toronto Press, 1962), 294 pp.; *Understanding Media, the Extensions of Man* (New York: McGraw-Hill Book Company, 1964), 360 pp.

50. "Universities and their Function," p. 147.

51. Carroll V. Newsom, *A University President Speaks Out: on Current Education* (New York: Harper & Brothers, 1961), p. 4, said: "Unless a teacher provides the stimulation

necessary to start the intellectual machinery within his students, he is a doubtful success. The creation of an atmosphere where people will want to think and then will think is the challenge to every person who wants to be known as a 'teacher.'"

52. *Democracy and Education* (New York: The Macmillan Company, 1916), pp. 311-323; *Experience and Education* (New York: The Macmillan Company, 1938), 116 pp.

53. "The Academic Career: Notes on Recruitment and Colleagueship," *Daedalus*, LXXX-VIII (Winter 1959), pp. 147-169; reprinted in a condensed version under title of "The College Professor," in Brand Blanshard, editor, *Education in the Age of Science* (New York: Basic Books, Inc. 1959), pp. 263-284. See also Riesman's article, "Law and Sociology: Recruitment, Training, and Colleagueship," *Stanford Law Review*, IX (July 1957), 643-673.

54. "The Academic Career," p. 168, n. 15. See also Everett C. Hughes, *Men and Their Work* (Glencoe, Illinois: The Free Press, 1958), pp. 47, 106-109.

55. "The Academic Career," p. 161.

56. Maurice Merleau-Ponty (1907-1961), *Phenomenology of Perception,* in the translation of Colin Smith (New York: The Humanities Press, 1962), p. 354.

57. The words are those of Wilfrid Ward in the "Introduction" to the Everyman's Library edition of Newman's *On the Scope and Nature*

of University Education, p. xiii. The context in which they occur is: "The work of discriminating is arduous, and can only be done by learned men. It must be a work of time, it cannot be extemporized to meet an emergency. A university with its continuous life of thought and learning is just the machinery that is required. It is not a court which is called upon to hear evidence and decide at a moment of crisis; it is an ever-living, ever-working machine which is constantly at work on these problems and has first-rate experts at its disposal."

58. *The Republic of Science, Its Political and Economic Theory*, a lecture delivered at Roosevelt University, January 11, 1962 (Chicago: Roosevelt University, 1962), 27 pp.

59. *Ibid.*, p. 25.

60. *Chaim Weizmann* (New York: Farrar, Straus, and Cudahy, 1958), p. 3.

61. *The Uses of the University*, pp. 91-94.

62. *The House of Intellect* (New York: Harper & Brothers, 1959), 276 pp.

63. "The Frantic Race to Remain Contemporary," p. 1055.

64. Josiah Royce (1855-1916), *The Problem of Christianity*, 2 volumes (New York: The Macmillan Company, 1913), II, 313, 325; *The Philosophy of Loyalty* (New York: The Macmillan Company, 1908), pp. 252-258. See also Gabriel Marcel, *Royce's Metaphysics*, in the translation of Virginia and Gordon Ringer

(Chicago: Henry Regnery Company, 1956), pp. 112-113.

65.   *The Mystery of Being,* 2 volumes (Chicago: Henry Regnery Company, 1960), I, "Reflection and Mystery," Gifford Lectures of 1949, pp. 89-92.

66.   Jacob E. Cooke, editor (Middletown, Connecticut: Wesleyan University Press, 1961), numbers 10, 62, 47, 37, 51. In summary, the dangers are: 1) The spirit of party and faction, which is so clearly the natural and necessary offspring of tendencies always present in mankind that it must be looked for wherever liberty exists. 2) The propensity of legislators to yield to the impulse of sudden and violent passion, and to be seduced by factious leaders into intemperate and pernicious resolutions. 3) Mutability in the public councils arising from a rapid succession of new members. 4) The propensity of the legislative department to intrude upon the rights, and to absorb the powers, of the other departments. 5) The propensity of the general government to take over the functions of the local (state) governments. 6) Oppression of the minority by the majority.

67.   *The Mystery of Being,* I, 90.

68.   Quoted by Clark Kerr, "The Frantic Race to Remain Contemporary," p. 1051. See also John W. Gardner, "The Future of the University," *Saturday Review,* November 2, 1963, p. 46; David Starr Jordan, "University-Building," *Popular Science Monthly,* LXI (August 1902), 330-338.

69. Remarks of Donald Michael, published in *The Environment of Change,* a Conference at Sterling Forest, Tuxedo, New York, June 14-17, 1964, pp. 35-37.

70. Robert Maynard Hutchins' phrase in his Charles R. Walgreen Foundation lectures, *The University of Utopia* (Chicago: The University of Chicago Press, 1953), 103 pp.

The Aquinas Lectures

Published by the Marquette University Press,
Milwaukee 3, Wisconsin

St. Thomas and the Life of Learning (1937) by John F. McCormick, S.J., (1874-1943) professor of philosophy, Loyola University.

St. Thomas and the Gentiles (1938) by Mortimer J. Adler, Ph.D., director of the Institute of Philosophical Research, San Francisco, Calif.

St. Thomas and the Greeks (1939) by Anton C. Pegis, Ph.D., professor of philosophy, Pontifical Institute of Mediaeval Studies, Toronto.

The Nature and Functions of Authority (1940) by Yves Simon, Ph.D., (1903-1961) professor of philosophy of social thought, University of Chicago.

St. Thomas and Analogy (1941) by Gerald B. Phelan, Ph.D., professor of philosophy, St. Michael's College, Toronto.

St. Thomas and the Problem of Evil (1942) by Jacques Maritain, Ph.D., professor *emeritus* of philosophy, Princeton University.

Humanism and Theology (1943) by Werner Jaeger, Ph.D., Litt.D., (1888-1961) University professor, Harvard University.

The Nature and Origins of Scientism (1944) by
John Wellmuth.

Cicero in the Courtroom of St. Thomas Aquinas
(1945) by E. K. Rand, Ph.D., Litt.D., LL.D.,
(1871-1945) Pope professor of Latin, *emeritus*, Harvard University.

St. Thomas and Epistemology (1946) by Louis-Marie Regis, O.P., Th.L., Ph.D., director of
the Albert the Great Institute of Mediaeval
Studies, University of Montreal.

St. Thomas and the Greek Moralists (1947,
Spring) by Vernon J. Bourke, Ph.D., professor of philosophy, St. Louis University, St.
Louis, Missouri.

History of Philosophy and Philosophical Education (1947, Fall) by Étienne Gilson of the
Académie française, director of studies and
professor of the history of Mediaeval philosophy, Pontifical Institute of Mediaeval Studies,
Toronto.

The Natural Desire for God (1948) by William
R. O'Connor, S.T.L., Ph.D., former professor of
dogmatic theology, St. Joseph's Seminary,
Dunwoodie, N.Y.

St. Thomas and the World State (1949) by
Robert M. Hutchins, former Chancellor of the
University of Chicago, president of the Fund
for the Republic.

Method in Metaphysics (1950) by Robert J. Henle, S.J., Ph.D., dean of the graduate school, St. Louis University, St. Louis, Missouri.

Wisdom and Love in St. Thomas Aquinas (1951) by Étienne Gilson of the *Académie française*, director of studies and professor of the history of Mediaeval philosophy, Pontifical Institute of Mediaeval Studies, Toronto.

The Good in Existential Metaphysics (1952) by Elizabeth G. Salmon, Ph.D., professor of philosophy in the graduate school, Fordham University.

St. Thomas and the Object of Geometry (1953) by Vincent Edward Smith, Ph.D., director, Philosophy of Science Institute, St. John's University.

Realism and Nominalism Revisited (1954) by Henry Veatch, Ph.D., professor of philosophy, Indiana University.

Imprudence in St. Thomas Aquinas (1955) by Charles J. O'Neil, Ph.D., professor of philosophy, Villanova University.

The Truth That Frees (1956) by Gerard Smith, S.J., Ph.D., professor and chairman of the department of philosophy, Marquette University.

St. Thomas and the Future of Metaphysics (1957) by Joseph Owens, C.Ss.R., Ph.D., professor of philosophy, Pontifical Institute of Mediaeval Studies, Toronto.

Thomas and the Physics of 1958: A Confrontation (1958) by Henry Margenau, Ph.D., Eugene Higgins professor of physics and natural philosophy, Yale University.

Metaphysics and Ideology (1959) by Wm. Oliver Martin, Ph.D., professor of philosophy, University of Rhode Island.

Language, Truth and Poetry (1960) by Victor M. Hamm, Ph.D., professor of English, Marquette University.

Metaphysics and Historicity (1961) by Emil L. Fackenheim, Ph.D., professor of philosophy, University of Toronto.

The Lure of Wisdom (1962) by James D. Collins, Ph.D., professor of philosophy, St. Louis University.

Religion and Art (1963) by Paul Weiss, Ph.D. Sterling professor of philosophy, Yale University.

St. Thomas and Philosophy (1964) by Anton C. Pegis, Ph.D., professor of philosophy, Pontifical Institute of Mediaeval Studies, Toronto.

The University In Process (1965) by John O. Riedl, Ph.D., professor of philosophy, Marquette University.

Uniform format, cover and binding.